CULTURE
in Singapore

Melanie Guile

Heinemann
LIBRARY

 www.heinemann.co.uk/library
Visit our website to find out more information about Heinemann Library books.

To order:
☎ Phone 44 (0) 1865 888066
🖹 Send a fax to 44 (0) 1865 314091
💻 Visit the Heinemann Bookshop at www.heinemann.co.uk/library to browse our catalogue and order online.

First published 2003 in Australia by Heinemann Library a division of Harcourt Education Australia, 18–22 Salmon Street, Port Melbourne Victoria 3207 Australia (a division of Reed International Books Australia Pty Ltd, ABN 70 001 002 357).

Series cover and text design by Stella Vassiliou
Paged by Stella Vassiliou
Edited by Carmel Heron
Production by Michelle Sweeney

Pre-press by Digital Imaging Group (DIG), Melbourne, Australia
Printed and bound in China by WKT Company Ltd.

ISBN 1 74070 133 X (hardback)
08 07 06 05 04 03
10 9 8 7 6 5 4 3 2 1

ISBN 0 431 18132 2 (paperback)
09 08 07 06 05
10 9 8 7 6 5 4 3 2 1

British Library Cataloguing in Publication Data
Guile, Melanie.
Culture in Singapore.
306'.095957
A full catalogue record for this book is available from the British library.

Acknowledgements
Cover image of parade in Tang Dynasty Living History Museum, Singapore, supplied by Australian Picture Library/Corbis/© James Marshall.

Other photographs supplied by: Australian Picture Library (APL): pp. 6 (bottom), 7, 11, 13, 16, 17, 29; AFP/AAP/Roslan Rahman: p. 8; APL/Corbis/© David Reed: p. 14; Blake Chen: p. 19; Courtesy of Su Chen Christine Lim: p. 23; MediaCorp TV: p. 25; Courtesy of the National Archives of Singapore: pp. 6 (top), 9, 10, 18, 20; The Nostalgia Factory: p. 24; *Still Life: Moon Festival Table* by Georgette Chen: p. 27 and *Girl with Folded Arms* by Chong Fah: p. 28, both Courtesy of the Singapore Art Museum; Courtesy of the Singapore Tourism Board: p. 12; Courtesy of TheatreWorks: p. 21; Daniel Yam Fashions photograph by Steve Wood: p. 15.

Every attempt has been made to trace and acknowledge copyright. Where an attempt has been unsuccessful, the publisher would be pleased to hear from the copyright owner so any omission or error can be rectified in subsequent printings.

CONTENTS

Words that appear in bold, **like this**, are explained in the glossary on page 30.

CULTURE IN *Singapore*

A dot on the map

On a map of the world, Singapore is a tiny dot off the tip of the Malay **peninsula**. It is a small island nation surrounded by much larger neighbours, Indonesia and Malaysia.

Singapore has no natural wealth or productive land to farm or mine. It is a young country – 200 years ago the island was a swampy jungle – and its 4.13 million people come from all over Asia. Yet today, Singapore is one of the world's great cities – modern, wealthy and proud.

The melting pot of Singapore

The secret of Singapore's success is its key position on the world's busiest trading route. The Englishman Sir Stamford Raffles signed a treaty with the **indigenous** Malays and founded a trading port in 1819 on behalf of the British East India Trading Company. Malay people from the mainland flocked to work in the port. Migrants from South China poured in to take the hard labouring jobs on the wharfs, and the settlement boomed. Wealthy Chinese merchants, many of them **Peranakans**, or Straits Chinese, from Malaya, built **shophouses** on the quay and started thriving businesses. English government officials came and brought Indians and Sri Lankans to work with them. Soon, the city was a **melting pot** of different races and cultures.

For many years, the different **ethnic groups** preserved their own traditions and there was no distinctively Singaporean culture. But since independence in 1965, the government has worked hard to give the people a sense of common goals and values within this **multicultural** society.

Shared values

In multicultural Singapore, the government encourages its citizens to identify as Singaporean. The official 'five shared values' are:
- nation before community
- the importance of family
- respect for the individual
- **consensus** not conflict
- racial and religious harmony.

What is culture?

Culture is a people's way of living. It is the way a group of people identifies itself as separate and different from any other. Culture includes a group's spoken and written language, social customs and habits, as well as its traditions of art, craft, dance, drama, music, literature and religion.

But what does culture mean in Singapore, where the Chinese (77 per cent of the population), the Malays (14 per cent), the Indians (8 per cent) and the English (1 per cent) have left their cultural mark, as have Arab traders and islanders from Indonesia? Where do you find the unique culture of Singapore?

Designed by a government committee in 1959, Singapore's flag captures the nation's commitment to peace and harmony. The red stands for brotherhood and equality, the white represents purity and goodness. The moon represents a new country on the rise and the stars stand for the nation's five ideals: democracy, peace, progress, justice and equality.

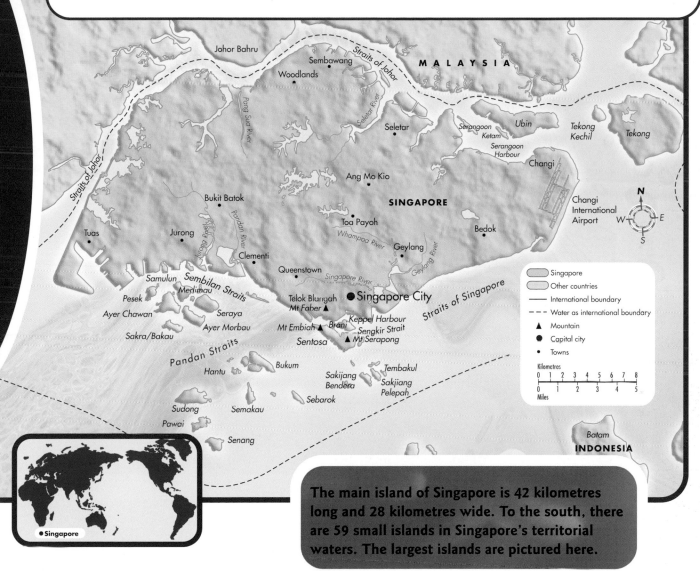

The main island of Singapore is 42 kilometres long and 28 kilometres wide. To the south, there are 59 small islands in Singapore's territorial waters. The largest islands are pictured here.

You find it in the up-beat, success-oriented mood of the gleaming downtown malls, crammed with the latest hi-tech goods and clothes from all over the world. You find it in the many churches, temples, shrines and **mosques** serving the spiritual needs of the **Christians**, **Buddhists**, **Hindus** and **Muslims** in the city. You will certainly find it in the mouth-watering smells coming from the **hawkers**' market stalls, which earn Singapore the label of food capital of Asia. You will hear it in the rapid-fire English **dialect** called '**Singlish**', with its sprinkling of Malay and Chinese words. And you will sense it in the restless need of the people always to get ahead, to succeed, not to lose out, which Singaporeans call *kiasu*.

Traditional and modern

Amid the fast-paced life of modern Singapore, pockets of older traditions survive. The city is famous for its hundreds of religious and cultural festivals as each ethnic community celebrates its ancient traditions. **Dialects** from south China can still be heard among Chinatown's older residents, in spite of government campaigns to encourage the use of the official **Mandarin** Chinese language. **Peranakan**, or Straits Chinese, families still display their wealth in lavish weddings, and use their own Peranakan language at home. Rows of old terraced **shophouses** line Chinatown streets in the shadow of high-rise office buildings.

Yet Singapore is searching for symbols of its own, such as the official mascot the Merlion, a lion head with a fish's body (symbolising courage, strength and excellence) and the national flower, a pink and white orchid chosen in 1981 for its adaptability and toughness. With 'new' symbols like these, the government hopes to build a unique, distinctly Singaporean culture.

Terraced shophouses built by Chinese merchants in the 1800s. The shopfronts are at street level with living quarters above.

Flush or fine

The government is proud of its spotless public places and enforces cleanliness with S$1000 fines for smoking, littering or not flushing the toilet in its 'flush or fine' campaign. Other successes include campaigns on birth control, speaking Mandarin Chinese, and encouraging acts of kindness among citizens with the Singapore Kindness Movement.

Singapore's national flower, the pink and white orchid.

The good life

Life is good for modern Singaporeans. After years of hard work, the population is reaping its rewards. Wages are high and almost everyone has a job. The government's Housing and Development Board (HDB) provides accommodation in high-rise flats for all, and most people (93 per cent) own their own apartments. Good health care and education are available, and most people retire on generous pension payments. Women have more freedom and opportunity here than in many other parts of Asia. The crime rate is low and the city is safe, clean and well serviced.

It is not all positive, however. In spite of Singapore's reputation for peaceful **multiculturalism, ethnic groups** still view each other warily and most people marry within their own communities. The dominance of Chinese culture threatens to overwhelm the smaller ethnic groups, particularly the **indigenous** Malays. The strong government control over every aspect of Singaporean life impacts on artists, politicians and highly educated intellectuals whose calls for more freedom are quickly stifled. But, for most people, the welfare of the group or society is more important than individual happiness, and Singaporeans generally are content with their strictly controlled society.

The Merlion, the lion-headed logo of Singapore.

The cost of speaking out

Singapore is a peaceful society but that comes at a cost. Power is held by one party (the People's Action Party), which permits only a few token **opposition** members, so voters have no real choice of who governs them. Any criticism of the government is viewed as dangerous and antisocial. Leader of the Opposition Chee Soon Juan was fined over S$1 million and banned from politics for five years in 2002 when he was found guilty of **defaming** Prime Minister Goh Chok Tong and former Prime Minister Lee Kuan Yew. He had accused them of providing loans to **corrupt** states. Only six months before, another opposition politician suffered the same fate.

TRADITIONS
and customs

East meets west

Ultra-modern in so many ways, Singapore still maintains many of the traditions and customs of the main groups who formed it – the Malays, Chinese, English and Indians. Westerners may be surprised to learn, for example, that businessmen often ask a **feng shui** expert to arrange the furniture in an office building to bring maximum luck and money to the business. Orchard Road lights up for Christmas, while Little India sparkles during the **Hindu** Festival of Light, *Deepavali*. In the cultural mix of Singapore, traditions from east and west are recognised by all.

Paper lantern on display at the Chinese Mid-Autumn Festival. This is traditionally a Chinese harvest festival, but in Singapore it is known for its decorated lantern competitions.

Social graces

Although Singaporean life is becoming more casual, in line with western trends, there is still an Asian formality about the way Singaporean people mix. Generally, people are polite, restrained and a little reserved, and loud, unruly behaviour is uncommon. 'Saving face' (not being shamed or humiliated) is very important, and it is rude to openly disagree with or contradict someone else.

Children are expected to show respect to their parents and look after them when they get old, although it is unusual now for young couples to live with their in-laws. Acceptance and tolerance are encouraged, and for the most part, Singaporeans do not like to criticise or challenge their superiors.

Songbirds on Sundays

The sweet sound of hundreds of songbirds can be heard on Sunday mornings in parks around the city – but these birds are not in the trees. Bird fanciers gather together with their caged songbirds to meet, drink tea and showcase the musical skills of their pet songsters.

Chinese New Year

Chinese New Year is the country's major festival. It is held during January or February (depending on the **lunar calendar**). For weeks beforehand, families pay off debts, clean their houses and buy new clothes. Red posters with good wishes in Chinese are pinned up, and Chinatown is decked with decorations of plum blossom and **kumquat trees**. A family dinner is held on New Year's Eve when children are given little red packets of money (*hong bao*) for luck.

On New Year's Day, people visit relatives and friends, and lion or dragon dances are performed in the streets. Traditionally, firecrackers were also used to scare off bad spirits, but the government has now banned them for safety reasons.

The holiday season ends on the Sunday after New Year with the spectacular *Chingay* street parade (started in 1973), featuring plays of Chinese **myths**, stilt walkers and huge, lavish floats.

Perfomers in the *Chingay* street parade, which marks the end of the New Year holiday season.

Chinese calendar

The Chinese calendar runs on a 12-year cycle known as the Chinese zodiac. Each year is allotted a different animal. The year of the dragon is especially lucky. Here is the zodiac for the current cycle:

1996 – Rat	2000 – Dragon	2004 – Monkey
1997 – Ox	2001 – Snake	2005 – Rooster
1998 – Tiger	2002 – Horse	2006 – Dog
1999 – Rabbit	2003 – Goat	2007 – Pig

Religious festivals

Although Singapore has a mainly Chinese population, other **ethnic groups** are encouraged to observe their own customs and traditions. That's why the calendar is crammed with a huge variety of religious festivals – Indian **Hindu** celebrations, **Buddha's** Birthday, **Islamic** and **Christian** holidays, and Chinese feasts and festivals.

Deepavali – *Festival of Lights*

This major Hindu festival celebrates the victory of good over evil and light over darkness. For *Deepavali*, Little India is ablaze with lights, and statues of the gods are carried through the streets. Families set oil lamps to help the souls of the dead back to the other world, and children are given special treats at this happy time.

Thaipusam

A very different, solemn Hindu festival is *Thaipusam*, in honour of Lord Muruga, god of bravery, power and goodness. Men imitate the god's bravery by enduring intense pain. Pins, chains and spikes are driven through their skin and attached to large cage-like structures (called *kavadis*), which they carry on their shoulders through the streets to the temple.

A religious man endures skin piercing as he walks in a trance to the temple at the festival of *Thaipusam*. The cage-like *kavadi* he carries is decorated with peacock feathers and food offerings to the Lord Muruga.

Buddhists lighting incense for the *Vesak* Day celebrations.

Vesak *Day*

Vesak Day celebrates the birthday of Buddha, the founder of the **Buddhist** religion. Statues of Buddha are washed at dawn, prayers are recited and temples are decorated with flags, flowers and lanterns. This is a time of giving (*dana*) for Singaporean Buddhists, who give money to the poor, visit hospitals and prisons, and donate blood. The celebration ends with candle-lit processions to temples and the chanting of verses (*sutras*).

Hari Raya Puasa

Muslims do not eat from sunrise to sunset during the holy month of Ramadan, to learn compassion for the poor by going hungry. The festival of *Hari Raya Puasa* celebrates 'openness of mind and heart' to mark the end of this time of hunger. It begins with asking forgiveness from the family, and visits to the mosque. Friends get together and celebrate with special food, including *rendang* (spicy stew) and *ketupat* (rice cooked in woven coconut leaves). Singaporean Muslims often invite non-Muslims to join the festivities in the spirit of openness that marks the season.

Hungry ghosts

Around August each year in Singapore you will see small paper houses, cars and clothes set down on roadsides. These are offerings to please the dead, whose spirits walk the Earth during the month of the Chinese Festival called the Feast of Hungry Ghosts. Special food is also prepared at home and offered to the ghosts. Once they have been satisfied, the family eats the banquet.

11

PERANAKAN *culture*

The people

For over 400 years, the **Peranakan**, or Straits Chinese, have thrived as a distinct and successful **ethnic group** in the region. The culture arose long ago when Chinese merchants married Malay women and established a way of life that borrowed from both traditions. Peranakan means 'born locally' in Malay. Peranakan *babas* (men) and *nonyas* (women) have their own language, **cuisine**, costumes and customs but, like most ethnic groups today, they struggle to preserve this unique identity.

A comfortable life

Peranakans have always been good business people. Unlike other traders in early Singapore, they spoke Chinese, Malay and often English, giving them an advantage over business rivals. By the 1800s, they were building **shophouses** in Chinatown and fine mansions in the better suburbs.

Peranakans led a stylish and wealthy lifestyle. They sent their children to private schools. Their large, airy houses (called *rumah*) were filled with ornate carved furniture, often inlaid with mother-of-pearl. They held lavish feasts for hundreds of guests, eating from brightly decorated porcelain (china) plates. Entertainments included European sports like tennis and golf, gambling and cards. *Cherki*, a complex card game, is still played in the Peranakan community.

Peranakan furnishings show a mix of Chinese and European styles.

Costume

Rich silks in brilliant colours, ornate embroidery and lavish beading are the hallmarks of Peranakan costumes. Traditionally, men wore loose Chinese jackets and trousers, and women wore Malay dress (**sarong kebaya**). *Nonyas* wore finely embroidered and beaded shoes called *kasut manek*, and loved to wear extravagant jewellery. Bangles, tiaras, neck pendants and earrings were popular. Most jewellery was silver inlaid with precious stones, and often decorated in Chinese style with flowers, butterflies and dragons.

On special occasions such as weddings and festivals, these traditional costumes are still worn, along with extravagant silver headpieces. Many older Peranakan women still wear the graceful *sarong kebaya* for everyday use.

Leaders of the community

Wealthy and educated, the Peranakans have had a major influence on life in Singapore. The first Chinese language newspaper in Singapore, *Lat Pau*, was started by a Peranakan, See Ewe Lay in 1881 and ran for 52 years. *Nonyas* took a leading role in fighting for women's freedom and the right to vote. Peranakan politicians and business leaders have helped shape the nation since independence in 1965. The nation's first Prime Minister Lee Kuan Yew was a third-generation Peranakan. Today in Singapore, Peranakan community organisations are dedicated to making sure this unique culture is not lost.

Feeling blue

Peranakan clothing, porcelain and homewares are famous for their brilliant colours, but blue is not among them. Peranakans wear blue at funerals, and the colour is associated with death and sadness.

COSTUME
and clothing

Western gear

Singapore is a modern city and its shops are crammed with the latest fashions. But look more closely and you will find evidence of Singapore's rich cultural mix in the clothes its people wear.

Traditional costumes

Traditional Chinese women's wear is the *cheong sam*, a long, fitted dress made of silk. Men traditionally wore loose trousers and a soft jacket. In the 1800s, a long pigtail called a *queue* was compulsory for men in China but not in Singapore, so migrants cut theirs off as soon as they arrived. Today, Chinese-Singaporean women wear the *cheong sam* only on special occasions like Chinese New Year. Indian-Singaporean women, however, can still be seen wearing *saris* – the traditional dress of southern India made of one long strip of material draped around the body.

Malay-Singaporean women commonly wear the **sarong kebaya** for everyday use. This is a fitted blouse (often of lace) and long skirt made of **batik**. Malay men sometimes wear the traditional *baju melayu* (jacket, black hat and loose trousers), or may wear the hat with their business suits.

Malay-Singaporean women commonly wear the traditional *sarong kebaya*, made famous as the uniform worn by Singapore Airlines flight attendants.

New-fashioned ideas

Singaporean fashion designers are beginning to make an international impact. Styles tend to be soft and flowing, and beautiful evening wear in rich fabrics are a specialty.

Celia Loe was a pioneer in local design in the 1970s, making her name with affordable, high-quality and fashionable clothes. Her women's business suits with huge shoulder pads made her famous throughout Asia. Benny Ong is known for his beautiful evening gowns worn by Princess Diana. Daniel Yam designs sleek, sophisticated clothes using tie-dyed fabrics in unusually subtle colours.

Government-run events like Singapore Fashion Week, local colleges of design, and facilities for buying fashion items on the Internet, all aim to encourage this newly emerging local industry.

The modern Singapore 'look' by young fashion designer Daniel Yam.

Cool powder

Peranakan *nonyas* (women) traditionally wore face powder made of soaked and perfumed rice, which was ground up and moulded into small cakes. This cosmetic was called *bedak sejok* (cool powder) because of its cooling effect in the tropical heat.

FOOD

Eating out is a national pastime in Singapore, and downtown streets are crammed with eateries selling food from all over the world. The original Malay inhabitants, **Peranakan** merchants, migrant Chinese and Indians, and government officials from England all brought their own cooking styles to make Singapore a gourmet's delight.

Malay food

Spicy prawn paste, tangy lemon grass and creamy coconut milk form the basis of Malay food. Lamb, beef and chicken (sometimes cooked on skewers as *satay*) are popular served with peanut sauce. *Sambal*, a prawn and hot chilli flavouring, is a key ingredient in many popular dishes. Malay cooking does not use pork because it is forbidden in the **Islamic** religion. *Laksa* is a thick soup of rice noodles in coconut milk with soybean curd, vegetables, chicken and seafood. An elaborate dish is *ketupat*, in which rice is cooked in parcels of woven coconut leaves.

Malay satay, Indian curry and Chinese chicken on offer for a Singaporean meal.

Nonya *cuisine*

Nonya – the Peranakan word for 'woman' – gives its name to Singapore's most distinctive cooking style – a mix of Malay and Chinese tastes. Fragrant spices blend with milder Chinese flavours in traditional *Nonya rempah*, which is a flavouring made up of ground chillis, garlic, spring onions, lemon grass, turmeric, and prawn paste (*belacan*). Specialty dishes include *otak-otak*, made of fish, coconut milk, chilli paste and herbs wrapped in a banana leaf; and *itek tim*, a soup with duck, salted vegetables and pickled plums. Peranakans are **Christian** or **Buddhist**, so pork is eaten, and strong, meaty pork and liver sausages (*hati babi*) are popular. *Nonya* desserts are very sweet, sticky and delicious.

Cheap and delicious Asian food is available at popular **hawkers'** centres like this one. Every kind of **cuisine** – from fast-food stores to up-market Japanese and French restaurants – is available in Singapore.

Chinese

Most Chinese Singaporeans originally came from southern China, and the cooking styles of Sichuan, Canton and Hokkien are evident in the food available. There are the hot chilli flavours of Sichuan Province and the delicious **dim sum** from Canton. There is the *popiah* (turnip, prawn and bean–sprout spring rolls) and the *or luak* (oysters and fried egg dipped in chilli sauce) from the Hokkien province of China. Eating out at hawkers' centres is extremely popular among Chinese Singaporeans.

Indian food

Fiery curries with rice from south India and creamy *tandoori* dishes served with *naan* (bread) from north India are available from the eateries of Little India. Buddhists (from south India) do not eat animal products, so vegetarian cuisine is highly developed among these groups. Traditionally served on banana leaves and eaten with the fingers, Indian dishes are affordable and very tasty.

Hawkers' markets

Thousands of street hawkers used to sell food from carts in the city's lanes. To clean up the streets and improve food-handling practices, these were replaced in 1987 by hawkers' centres, which are government-run open-air food halls. Here, the same rich eating experience can be had without the risk of stomach upsets.

17

Finding a voice

In the years after independence, Singaporeans worked very hard to build a new nation. There was little time left over to enjoy the luxury of the performing arts – music, dance or theatre. But in the last few years this has changed. Today, creative artists and performers are finding a voice that is distinctly Singaporean.

Traditional music

Chinese opera came to Singapore with the first Chinese migrants nearly 200 years ago and is still staged today. Performers wear richly decorated robes and headpieces and act out age-old stories in a formal style. Costumes and make-up are used to express the nature of the characters and performers sing to the music of a traditional Chinese orchestra. The Chinese Opera Institute was established by the government in 1995 to promote this art form. Performances are held in parks and streets year round, and audiences cheer and boo the characters in the traditional way.

Chinese opera incorporates traditional music, singing, acting and dance.

The Singapore Chinese Orchestra (established in 1996) uses traditional Chinese instruments such as drums, gongs, bamboo flutes and zithers (stringed instruments). Its Millenium Concert in 2000 saw a record-breaking 1400 musicians take to the stage. The government sees traditional Chinese performing arts as an important part of the country's **heritage**.

Western classical music is also popular. The Singapore Symphony Orchestra showcases the talents of local musicians, and also attracts performers from around the world. European operas are staged by the Singapore Lyric Opera, a professional company that adapts classical European operas for the Asian context. A 2001 performance of the Italian composer Verdi's opera, *Il Travatore*, set the story in the Philippines with singers from Taiwan, Japan and Indonesia.

Rock and pop music

Bands with attitude have arrived on the local Singaporean music scene. Gone are the soppy love songs and tame pop-rock style of the old local outfits. Today's bands blend western sounds with local influences to produce a completely new sound.

Popular rock singer Blake Chen calls himself The Hungry Ghost. His latest gothic CD album features haunted-house sound effects such as echoes, creaks and electronic wind-howls. Rock band Force Vomit serves wilder tastes with their **alternative** punk-rock sound (locally called *Singa-alt* rock).

On the pop scene, Sun Yanzi has star status in Singapore. Her girlish looks and up-beat sound have won her awards at home and in Taiwan. Her 2001 hit single 'Cloudy Day' was a success all over the region. Another female pop star is singer–songwriter Tanya Chua. She records in English and **Mandarin** Chinese, and her voice has been compared with Alanis Morissette's. Multi–talented Pamela Oei is a solo singer–guitarist who also has her own band, Peculiar Remedies. She also starred in the successful locally produced film musical *Forever Fever*.

Gospel pop

The Reverend Ho Yeow-Sun, pastor of City Harvest Church, has an unusual way of inspiring her congregation. As a pop singer with the Decca label, she draws concert crowds of 10 000 fans, attracted by her spangly gear and flashy stage effects. Her eight-storey church in Singapore's west, complete with an underground theatre, has a following of 13 000 faithful.

Dance

Folk and traditional dances have always been performed among the different **ethnic groups** in Singapore – especially the Malays, Indians and Chinese – and these traditional dances are still enjoyed. But a new approach to dance is also emerging. The Singapore Dance Theatre (SDT) has won an international reputation for new ideas in classical and modern ballet. It was founded in 1988 by Anthony Then and Goh Soo Khim (the current Artistic Director). Internationally famous dance masters and designers (choreographers) have worked with the SDT, and it tours around the world.

Chinese dance traditions are reinterpreted and modernised by the Dance Ensemble Singapore, which combines acrobatics and **martial arts** skills with movement and music. Well known and respected throughout South-East Asia, their spectacular and athletic performances are also popular favourites at the National Day and *Chingay* street parades in the city. Their young dancers' group, Little Angels, has successfully performed in Turkey, France, Spain and New Zealand.

A performance by the internationally famous Singapore Dance Theatre.

The stage

The leading English-language theatre company in Singapore is TheatreWorks. Artistic director Ong Keng Sen is world famous for his brilliant and unusual stage productions, including plays and operas. His 1997 version of the famous Shakespeare play *King Lear* included Asian influences such as a Thai classical dancer, a Chinese opera singer and a Japanese *Noh* theatre actor in the lead role. Other new ideas include performances that use unusual or quirky locations around Singapore, for example, his production of the play *Destinies of Flowers in the Mirror*, which was performed inside an enormous public fountain. Ong Keng Sen has produced works in Europe, the USA and Australia and won many awards for his work.

Substation is an arts centre for young creative people that specialises in unusual and **experimental** work. It was set up by the remarkable Kuo Pao Kun, who established Singapore's first performing arts school back in 1965 after working in radio in Australia. For nearly 40 years he wrote and directed plays in both **Mandarin** Chinese and English, and promoted drama in Singapore. In 1989 his work for the theatre was recognised when he was awarded the Cultural Medallion, one of the government's highest honours. Kuo Pao Kun died of cancer in September 2002 at the age of 63.

Banned

Writers and performers were outraged in 2000 when the play *Talaq* was banned by the government after just two performances. **Islamic** groups apparently objected to the play about an unhappy **Muslim** marriage because they believed it gave the wrong impression of Islam. The ban caused many performing artists to call for **censorship** to be lifted in Singapore.

Beginnings

The earliest Singapore-based literature appeared in the pages of the *Straits Chinese Magazine*, which ran monthly from 1897 to 1907. This 'cultural journal', written in English, was set up by two **Peranakans** – Song Ong Siang and Lim Boon Keng – to showcase the writing talents and ideas of local people. It included poems, articles and short stories. English has been the language of choice for most Singaporean writers ever since, although the government now promotes and encourages literature written in **Mandarin** Chinese.

The father of Singaporean poetry

Singapore's most famous poet is Edwin Thumboo. He began writing in the 1950s and published his first book of poems, *Rib of Earth*, in 1956. A later volume, *If Gods Can Die* (1977), was highly praised. Thumboo writes on social issues, focusing on the political and cultural life of Singapore. His struggle to find a distinctively Singaporean style and voice in his poems has brought him many writers' awards as well as the Public Service Star in 1991 for his contribution to literature. He is a Professor of English at the National University of Singapore.

Singapore stories

Goh Poh Seng is one of Singapore's most admired and prolific writers. His many novels, including *If We Dream Too Long* (1976), are known internationally and have been translated into several languages. He was also one of the first to write stage plays in English for Singaporean audiences. In 1983, Goh was awarded the Singapore Cultural Medallion for his work.

Concrete poetry

Poems written to form the shape of the subject – for example, apples or umbrellas – are known as 'concrete poems'. Popular writer Grace Chia filled the pages of her successful first book, *Womango* (1998), with strong **feminist** themes and offbeat, concrete poems.

Author Christine (Su Chen) Lim has won international praise for her novels.

Christine (Su Chen) Lim was the first woman to win the Singapore Literature Prize in 1992, for her novel *Fistful of Colours*. It is a story about three young women in the Singaporean arts scene. Lim won a highly prized Fulbright Scholarship to the USA in 1997 and is a well-regarded spokesperson for women writers in Singapore.

Multicultural writing

Another successful writer is Lew Poo Chan, a poet who writes in Chinese under the pen-name Dan Ying. She received an award for her book *Poems of Taiji* (1979) and has also been translated into English. K. Elangovan writes in Tamil (an Indian language) and broke new ground when he produced a collection of poems titled *Transcreations* (1988), written in a mix of two languages (Tamil and English).

Muhammad Ariff Ahmad is a highly respected literary figure in Singapore. Since the 1950s, he has promoted Malay language and literature as a teacher, lecturer and writer of poetry and novels. In 1993, he received an award from the Malay Language Council of Singapore for his efforts to encourage Malay writers.

FILM
and television

Early film

The first full-length feature film was shot in Singapore in 1933. Titled *Laila Majnum*, it was a Malay love story based on *Romeo and Juliet*. The Shaw family pioneered film production in Singapore, setting up a studio in the city using local Malay opera performers as actresses. Dramas, love stories and horror movies proved popular and ensured the success of Shaw Productions. Their cinema chain thrives today throughout Malaysia and Singapore.

Now screening

World War II and the struggles for independence in the 1960s prevented filmmaking for many years, but in recent times the industry has revived. In 1998, the government set up the Singapore Film Commission to encourage film production and support local talent. Local re-makes of Hollywood hits are popular with filmmakers. Titles include *Forever Fever*, a uniquely Singaporean take on the 1970's disco hit *Saturday Night Fever*, complete with a John Travolta look-alike.

A scene from the Singaporean film *Forever Fever*, starring Adrian Pang. The film is also called *That's The Way I Like It*, and *Don't Call Me John Travolta*.

However, Singaporean-made films, with their lightweight plots, have not been a great success at home or overseas. Critics claim that the pursuit of profit over quality, plus strict government **censorship** restrictions, stifle creative talent in Singaporean films. It is not all bad news, though.

Young director Eric Khoo has gained the critics' approval with his first feature film *12 Storeys* about **misfits** living in a Singaporean block of flats. Popular actor Jack Neo wrote and directed the hit comedy *I Not Stupid*, which broke new ground by gently criticising aspects of Singaporean life. It is now an 18-part television series. **Experimental** art films are shown at the Substation Cultural Centre's 'Moving Images' screenings, an arts program that supports directors trying out new ideas.

A reel failure

At the 2001 Singapore International Film Festival, the judges concluded that the six short Singaporean films chosen to compete for prizes were all 'sub-standard', and no award was given. Local filmmaker Brandon Wee said the Singapore film scene so far had produced 'a wretched ... harvest'. However, young filmmakers like Eric Khoo and Jack Ng are improving the quality of local productions.

Television

The government controls what is shown on television. The Singapore Broadcasting Authority dictates that programs must promote 'family values' and 'moral standards'. Channel NewsAsia broadcasts current affairs to South-East Asia with polished style, but there is little room for independent reporting or criticism of the government. Those who do can be fined or banned.

Sneak preview

Satellite TV is banned in Singapore, but locals can get around this problem by catching a ferry to Indonesia. On weekends they flock to Batam – one of the Riau Islands, 20 kilometres south of Singapore – where they can watch the huge range of TV programs available via satellite – uncensored.

Situation comedies (sitcoms), light dramas, chat and game shows dominate the seven television channels, and up to 80 per cent of these are locally produced. A huge success is the sitcom '*Phua Chu Kang*' about a family of incompetent builders. The title role is played by comedian Gurmit Singh whose signature yellow gumboots are recognised all over Singapore. He also has his own chat show. Pierre Png, a local film actor who plays the lead's brother, has become a teenage heart-throb. Another popular English language program is the comedy *Under One Roof*, starring the chubby Moses Lim as Tan Ah Tek – a convenience-store operator who heads an offbeat, squabbling family. The government frowns on the slang dialogue ('**Singlish**') used in such sitcoms.

As in every other aspect of Singaporean life, **multiculturalism** is an important influence on the visual arts, which include sculpture, painting and print-making. Traditional art techniques such as Malay *batik* print-making, Chinese brush painting, and French portraiture are blended and reinvented by Singaporean artists to produce fresh, creative works.

However, freedom of expression is a burning issue in today's Singapore. The government's **licensing system**, overseeing all public arts and entertainment, strictly controls what artists may do.

Painting pioneers

Georgette Chen (1907–1993) was a pioneer Singaporean artist and is regarded as one of the most important. She is best known for her portraits, which seem to capture the subjects' inner feelings and characters. *Self Portrait* (1946) gives a striking impression of the artist's strong personality as well as her beauty. Other paintings express her love of nature and the ordinary things of life, like the festive table decorations in the charming study *Still Life: Moon Festival Table*. Chen was one of the artists who in the 1950s founded the distinctive *Nanyang* style of modern art that blended modern European painting ideas with Chinese traditional techniques and subjects.

Another important pioneer is Chen Wen Hsi. A famous and highly skilled **calligrapher** (Chinese character writer) and artist, he is best known for his paintings of animals and landscapes in a modern, **abstract** style. He helped develop the *Nanyang* style as shown in his famous painting *Sparrow in the Rice Field*, painted between 1940 and 1950.

Thomas Yo (born 1936) is strongly influenced by European painters. He is famous for his beautiful, partly abstract, boldly coloured landscapes in watercolour, oils and **collage**. Highly regarded both overseas and at home, he was awarded the Cultural Medallion for his art by the Singaporean government in 1984.

New directions

Singaporean artists are continuing to push the boundaries with new ideas. Doctor and artist Chng Nai Wee creates **mixed-media** artworks and sculptures using a variety of materials. Calling himself an 'artist–scientist', he uses **web-based** programs, human voices, videos, electric cables and lights. His work *The Spirituality of Perception* displays a pile of human eyeballs lit up from the inside. Chng Nai Wee was named Singaporean Young Artist of the Year in 1999.

Koh Nguang How (born in 1963) produces paintings that include felt-pen detailing and photographs of other artists painting. In 1988, he helped to set up the Artists Village, a place where young artists gather, work and experiment with new ideas.

Sculpture

The leading sculptor in Singapore today is Ng Eng Teng. Born in 1934, Ng studied art locally and in the UK. He is best known for his sensitive treatment of human figures. The bronze statue *Sitting Pretty* is admired for the graceful shape and pose of the woman.

Another much-loved sculptor is Chong Fah Chong (born 1946), a Singaporean **Peranakan** who migrated to Canada in 1991. He works mostly in wood and takes his subjects from nature and his own experiences. His most famous work is the finely carved *Girl with Folded Arms*, although his later works have become more **abstract**.

Chong Fah Chong's much admired sculpture, *Girl with Folded Arms*.

Younger sculptors are experimenting with new materials. S. Chandrasekaran (born 1959) applies paints and resin paste to cotton *saris* (Indian women's dresses) to explore his Indian background.

The government funds public sculptures in city parks and squares. A popular favourite is the *Swiss Marble Fountain* in the Botanical Gardens. It consists of a large ball of solid marble spinning around on a thin film of water. Passers-by can stop the ball by touching it, but left alone it continues to spin as if by magic.

Is it art?

Sculptor Faizal Fadil likes to use **found objects** in his sculptures. His *Study of Three Thermos* caused outrage when it was shown at the Singapore Sculpture Exhibition in 1991. The work consisted of three used thermos flasks found at a local flea market, much to the dismay of some local art-lovers.

Calligraphy – writing as an art form

The ancient skill of **calligraphy** turns writing into an art form. The traditional method of writing uses a soft brush and ink on rice paper, and the characters (words) are like pictures. The thickness, flow and style of every brush stroke is important and the skill takes years to learn. Good calligraphers are highly respected as artists in Singapore. Even today in Chinatown, professional calligraphers set up booths in the street and offer their skills to passers-by for a fee.

Batik painting

Batik print-making is an ancient Malay craft. Fabric is patterned with wax then dyed many times to produce attractive prints. But Jaafar Latiff (born in 1937) has taken *batik* to a higher artistic level. Using traditional Malay *batik* techniques, he creates modern abstract art. He uses bold and brilliant colours to beautiful effect in his *Wandering Series* of prints, which are on display in the Singapore Art Museum.

Public exposure

When artist Josef Ng lowered his swimming shorts in public in 1994 as part of an artistic performance, the government arrested and fined him. Respected writer and art critic Alfian Bin Sa'at wrote an open letter to the Singaporean government claiming its **censorship** cast a 'shadow over the arts community'. Ng chose to leave the country to continue his work in Bangkok.

29

GLOSSARY

abstract not easy to understand or not realistic

alternative different option. It can also describe any style of music or other art form that is very different from what already exists.

batik decorative fabric created by painting patterns onto cloth with melted wax, dyeing the cloth, then removing the wax

Buddha, the founder of the Buddhist religion, Gautama Buddha, or any depiction of him, such as a statue

Buddhist/Buddhism having to do with Buddhism, or a person who follows the Buddhist religion. Buddhism is a belief system originating in India and now practised worldwide, although primarily in Asian countries and cultures. Buddhists follow the teachings of the Buddha and strive for a peaceful state called enlightenment.

calligraphy ancient form of Chinese picture-writing using ink and a brush

censorship act of preventing people from expressing their ideas or opinions

Christian/Christianity having to do with Christianity, or a person who follows the Christian religion, the main religion in most Western countries. Christians believe in one God and follow the teachings of Jesus Christ, which are written in a holy book called the Bible.

collage form of art in which pieces of paper are glued to a surface

consensus coming to agreement

corrupt dishonest; tending to behave immorally or illegally, especially for personal gain

cuisine food

defaming attacking someone verbally so that their reputation is damaged

dialect language that is unique to a specific place or area, often a variation of a language that is much more widespread

dim sum morsels of steamed or fried food served hot in bamboo baskets

ethnic group people who share a specific culture, language and background

experimental never tried before or different from usual, often in reference to a kind of performance, film or artwork

feminist person, male or female, who supports rights for women and girls equal to those enjoyed by men and boys

feng shui the ancient Chinese custom of arranging living spaces to bring positive energies and good luck to the occupiers

found objects materials used for artwork just as they were found by the artist, such as ordinary household objects or items salvaged from the rubbish

hawkers people who sell goods or food in the street or from door to door

heritage set of cultural traditions, beliefs and accomplishments that a generation inherits from previous generations

Hindu/Hinduism   having to do with Hinduism, or a person who follows the Hindu religion. Hinduism is an extremely diverse religion that originated in India, in which followers worship many gods and believe in the rebirth of souls into new bodies after death.

indigenous   native to a country or region; original inhabitants

Islam   the Muslim religion, based on the teachings of the prophet Mohammed

kumquat tree   a small citrus (orange-like) tree

licensing system   the Public Entertainment Licensing Unit (PELU) is a government agency that requires all forms of public and arts entertainment to obtain government permission before operating. Licences are compulsory and can be withdrawn at any time. This system is enforced by the police.

lunar calendar   calendar based on the intervals between new moons

Mandarin   language that originated in the north of China; the official language of Singapore

martial arts   traditional sports derived from hand-to-hand fighting techniques, for example judo, *tai chi* or kickboxing

melting pot   many different things blended together

misfits   people who do not fit into society

mixed media   artwork that uses a number of different materials together, such as paint, clay, fabric, wire and so on

mosques   places of prayer and worship in the Islamic religion

multicultural   made up of many cultures

Muslims   followers of Islam, a religion that is especially common in the Middle East and some parts of Asia. Muslims worship a single god called Allah and follow Allah's teachings, which were spread by the prophet Mohammed and are written about in a holy book called the Koran.

myths   ancient stories that usually explain how aspects of the world (or the world itself) came to be

Nanyang   style of art developed in the 1950s combining European painting ideas with traditional Chinese techniques and subjects

opposition   state of being against something; in politics, the opposition is a political party (or member of a political party) that hopes to replace the political party in power

peninsula   thin strip of land projecting from the mainland

Peranakans   ethnic group in Singapore and the Malay peninsula that came about over 400 years ago when Chinese merchants and indigenous Malays married together and had families; also known as Straits Chinese

sarong kebaya   traditional dress for Malay women; full-length wrap-around skirt worn with a long-sleeved fitted jacket

shophouses   terraced buildings of two or three storeys consisting of shops at street level and dwellings above

Singlish   common slang in Singapore that combines English and Mandarin words

web-based   from the Internet

INDEX